Resilience, R Safeguarding introduction for Childhood Studies

CW00420963

Rob Creasy

DEDICATION

To Fi as always for her contribution and insight.

CONTENTS

Resilience, Risk and Safeguarding

ACKNOWLEDGMENTS

How it ended up in this format owes much to the erudite discussions held over lunch at York St John University and the wise words of Julian Stern, Tony Leach & Jeff Buckles

1 RESILIENCE

1.1 Why is resilience important?

In recent years a concern with wellbeing has become very important. I explain what this is and why it is important in the associated book to this one, Wellbeing, Vulnerability and Life-chances, (Creasy 2020). In that book I talked about the way in which it is also important to consider the importance of understanding the concept of discourse. Discourse is explained further below but for now it is enough to know that it is bound up with how our ideas about the world, such as what is normal or obvious come to be accepted as such. One thing that you might consider at this point then is that some ideas can be said to be very seductive. Wellbeing is one of those seductive terms. Who wouldn't want children to experience wellbeing? You can see how it's what we might call a no-brainer.

But, if we want children to experience wellbeing then we also have to consider what contributes to that. In the book Wellbeing, Vulnerability and Life-chances I explained how it is that the broader context of childhood can act to make some children more vulnerable than others and then went on to consider how this fits in with a discussion of life-chances and inequalities. For example, later on in this book I will indicate how parental substance abuse is often automatically assumed to make things worse for children who live with them. It might, but it won't automatically or inevitably make things worse.

One key aspect of achieving wellbeing is the ability to be resilient, which is the focus of this chapter. At a basic level, resilience can be perceived as any individual's ability to deal with adversity. That might be dealing with problems as they happen or it could be overcoming them as we move forward , (Garrett, 2018,

Frydenberg, 2008). In looking at resilience in this way we can see how being resilient is important for our everyday life as we all encounter adversities in different shapes and forms just by being part of the social world. You could probably list a number of issues that have affected your life. I certainly could. If anything it is really difficult to imagine that any of us will not experience some adversity or setback at some point within our lives. It is important then that we are able to cope with adversity.

So, in a nutshell, we all need to be resilient and childhood and youth is a key time in our lives when we have experiences which contribute to how resilient we are. Very often though experiencing adversity is presented as something that is not good. Instead, and recognising that some adversities and situations can be unpleasant, I want you to consider how it is that experiencing some form of adversity is a crucial part of developing resilience. Look at it the other way around; if we never experience adversity, things which cause us a problem, then we can never really learn how to deal with the problems that we will inevitably face in our lives. This book explores three inter-related concepts, namely, risk, resilience and safeguarding to show how they all have some impact upon how childhood and youth are experienced.

1.2 What do we mean by resilience

We have to be careful when thinking about resilience because just like lots of other concepts relating to social life, we can see how it is a very slippery concept, (Martínez-Martí and Ruch, 2017, Ecclestone and Lewis, 2014, Taket et al., 2014). A concept can be referred to, or understood as slippery when they are hard to define or difficult to pin down. This is not at all unusual in social science because we are looking for a word which sums up something that is really quite complex. We might know what we mean by resilience but being confident that we all agree what we mean is not so easy. Because of this you might often find that some people use the term in slightly different ways. Don't worry about this. Just make sure that you always use it consistently.

When we think about the ways in which we understand resilience these tend to be dominated by ideas concerning an individual's character. This approach can be summarised by calling it a trait approach. Trait approaches used to be very popular with respect to explaining why some of us are more resilient than others. It was seen as something that we either had or didn't have.

More recent ideas about resilience however reject the idea that there is some inherent trait which means that we either are resilient or we are not. Instead we can see resilience as being the outcome of experiences or to see it in terms of being a process, (Fletcher and Sarkar, 2013). The main thing to consider though is that unless you experience some type of adversity it is hard to develop resilience. Think about it in terms of how we are protected against diseases by being given inoculations which give us a mild dose of a disease so that our bodies can develop resistance to it.

As you would expect with something that is so important a number of writers have explored issues to do with resilience and it is always useful to read a few sources to develop your own understanding. For example, Olsson et al. (2003), who are focused on adolescence, are useful in showing different ways in which we can understand resilience. With respect to this chapter they are useful because they also consider how wellbeing fits in to our understanding of resilience which is where we started. In addition though they also show how important it is to take social factors into consideration. In doing this they draw attention to the differences that are evident if we see resilience as an individual characteristic or trait that we can be said to possess compared to seeing it as a process.

When we start to see resilience as a process then we are drawn into understanding it in a broader sense. So, if we see resilience as a process rather than a characteristic that we may have, or that we may lack, we have to also recognise that it is not fixed. Instead we have to see it as something that is dynamic, (Hamilton, 2011).

If something is said to be dynamic it simply means that it is constantly changing. That doesn't mean that it is changing a lot just that it is changing to some extent. By recognising resilience as being dynamic we start to see how the extent to which we are resilient is always changing. So, if you think about yourself, by seeing resilience as a process you may recognise that there are some times and some situations wherein you are more resilient but there are other times when you are less resilient. This is a much better model that saying that we either have, or do not have, resilience.

With this in mind we then have to return to a consideration of what it is that might support our development of resilience or which may maintain the resilience that we have. At the same time we might start to see how individuals can become less resilient over time. This means that we have to think about the factors which can contribute to the ways in which we are able to build resilience, (Taket et al., 2014). Very often this can be seen as the outcome of the effect that three factors have on us. These three factors can be summed up as the individual, the family, and the community. As always though, a word of caution is appropriate.

These three factors may be the most influential of the factors which affect us in terms of developing and maintaining resilience but we don't experience them in a vacuum. We are also subject to other things which can have an impact upon us such as social policies at any given time, or the media. For example, think about how children and young people today are subject to pressures from social media that older people such as their parents or grandparents never experienced. This can create adversity in itself but it can also enhance support. So, if we take a broader view of the context in which any child or young people lives we should be able to have a much better understanding of why it is that some children will cope, but that others will seem to struggle even though the adversity that they face may appear to be the same.

1.3 The role of parents in developing resilience

What is not really in doubt is the importance of both developing and of maintaining resilience. However, in Wellbeing, Vulnerability and Life-chances it was argued that children are very often seen as being in some way, naturally vulnerable. If this is the case then we should also consider the role of parents in understanding resilience because children and young people tend to rely on parents to provide for them. I recognise that not all children and young people live with parents and that some adults who take on the role of parents are not, technically, their parents. As such an infant or young child may live apart from their parents for quite a number of years. For the purposes of simplicity though I will refer to parents as shorthand to mean parents and/or caregivers.

What parents do, particularly when it comes to what they do in the early years of a child's life will obviously have an influence upon how children develop. As such it may not be surprising to see that types of parenting styles that we may consider to be controlling or restrictive are associated with leading to children displaying low levels of resilience, (Taylor et al., 2013).

There are many factors which influence how a child develops. One factor is the extent to which a child is able to exert agency because what the child does will influence their individual experience and this will have some impact upon the extent to which they are able to develop and maintain resilience, (Hamilton, 2011). Remember that when we say agency in social science we are referring to any individual's capacity to act. To link back to the previous section though we should be aware that the political concerns of any government may increase or decrease the extent to which they are concerned with what happens within families, as well as greater or lesser concerns with the conditions within which families live.

1.4 Adversity and snowflakes

On the whole then you always need to be careful to consider how the concept of resilience is being defined and/or used in anything that you read. It is important and it is also clear that we all need some degree of resilience. We will all experience some form of adversity at some time and it is important that we are able to deal with it. Be careful though when you see or hear the concept of adversity being used. For example, there is a tendency at the moment to focus on adverse childhood experiences and to present these as the cause of later problems in adulthood. As always though we have to remember that child development is not simple. It is never a case of cause and effect. As an issue adverse childhood experiences have become quite important as a way of explaining why some children display social and emotional problems. However, Fergusson and Horwood (2003) demonstrate how it is that not all children with adverse experiences have problems. Always avoid falling in to the trap of being deterministic. It is the case that experiencing adverse childhood experiences can have an effect on children in their later lives but this is not bound to be the case.

The danger is in seeing adversity as both uniform, always the same, and of always being of major significance (Fletcher and Sarkar, 2013). We have already seen above that all children will experience adversity and that it is important that they do. In reality then, children will experience a range of adversities which we could classify as being low level.

So, instead of seeing adversity as being something or nothing, present or absent, and always bad, see it as something that is experienced as a continuum. By saying this I am saying that we must recognise that there are adversities that are quite minor and there are those that are much more significant. Think about the saying "first world problems". OK, you couldn't find your phone this morning but is that the same sort of problem as not having access to clean drinking water? Be careful also not to make the mistake of thinking that any child who experiences adverse childhood experiences will both be harmed or display long-lasting behaviour caused by it; they won't. Some may be, but many others will deal with it, often with support.

We all experience adversities as part of normal life and it is the case that for many reasons modern life can be stressful. We see evidence of what this means for children and young people in reports demonstrating increased levels of mental illness or decreased happiness. But think also about what you have read in this chapter. If we all need to experience adversity so as to develop and maintain resilience we can recognise how having our encounters with adversity reduced will have a knock-on effect on our ability to be resilient. In other words if we never face problems we never learn to deal with problems.

To end then, think about the term that is often used with respect to your generation if you are the typical 18 – 22 year old student; snowflakes. The term "snowflake" is used to refer to young people who are said to lack the ability to cope with criticism or stress, (Creasy and Corby, 2019). I am not claiming that the snowflake label is accurate. I am certainly not claiming that young people cannot handle stress, mainly because I think that the world is far more stressful now than it was when I was a young person. But, as a final thought, what if it is the case that young people cannot deal with stress or with criticism. Might it be because parents and other adults have sheltered them from it and therefore, they have never learnt how to deal with it? Could it be that in trying to remove all adversity from children and young people's lives as some parents seem to do, we have also reduced or removed opportunities to develop and maintain resilience? Together with Fiona Corby I explore this idea in Taming Childhood? A critical perspective on Parenting, Policy and Practice (Creasy and Corby, 2019) but the chapters on risk and safeguarding that follow will also be very useful if you want to explore this further.

1.5 What can I do with this?

My aim here is to provide a conclusion that illustrates how you might use this chapter. I will do this by picking out some key points that I think would be expected in an assignment on resilience. Bear in mind that your assignments may vary in what they are looking for and the marker may be looking for something very specific that I didn't cover. Always read your assignment guidance carefully and take advice about what is seen as a good assignment within your university. I place a great deal of importance on writing because the real task of a student is to demonstrate that you understand the material that you have covered. If you can explain a complicated theory or idea in a clear and simple way you will always look better yet students often make the mistake of thinking that the important thing is to cover the right material. OK, you might get the content right but if you don't write clearly then a lot of your effort will have gone to waste so get all the help that you can with writing and always make sure that you proof read and polish your assignments at least three times before submission.

But, with content in mind I think that an assignment on resilience really ought to make the point that:

- Resilience is important in that it contributes to wellbeing. This is important because you shouldn't just say that resilience is important you have to say why it is;

- Experiencing some form of adversity or challenge is a crucial part of developing resilience which means that if we remove all adversity from a child's life we are not helping them to develop resilience;

- When we see resilience as being rooted in individual character, something that we either have or lack then we can call it a trait;

- When we recognise that resilience is developed through experiences over time and that it has to be maintained we can see it as a process;

- If we see resilience as a process we can recognise that it is not fixed, it is dynamic;

- Three factors: the individual, the family, and the community, all contribute to developing resilience;

- Parenting styles can support or hold back the development of resilience;

When you write an assignment you will have to think about how you will introduce these points and make decisions about what order you cover them. Think about the context in which you use them. So, what point can you make? For example in Taming Childhood? Fiona Corby and I develop the argument that changes to parenting and practice that have been driven by worries about risk have meant that children and young people have fewer opportunities to develop resilience. You might think about how the points above fit in with this. You would then need to think about what you should read to be able to understand the issues. Use this book as the starting point and then think about how your reading provides you with the evidence (in the form of references) which will support your argument. Of course, what this also does is demonstrate how a concern with resilience is likely to mean that you also end up reading about risk. If so then the next chapter will be helpful.

2 RISK

2.1   Children, Risk & Resilience

As a student studying childhood or as a practitioner working with children and/or families you will be, or will inevitably come to be, familiar with the practice of making risk assessments. You will also probably be aware of limitations that are placed on children's activities because of risk. We seem to be living in a society where we are very conscious that things might go wrong and that children might be harmed. Just think about how many times, you will say, or it will be said to you, "take care". It seems innocuous really but the way in which "take care" has come to be a familiar farewell illustrates the way in which risk has come to be ever present in our everyday lives. With respect to children though there is a further issue to consider in that we are often driven by a concern that children should not be subject to risks and that they should not experience harm.

This chapter is focused on risk and it follows on from issues that were raised previously. In chapter 1 above it was argued that risks are important in respect of a child's development. Following from that, this chapter takes a critical approach to understanding risk and proposes that in actual fact, risk is an essential part of growing up. That is not to say that we should allow children and young people the freedom to do anything even though we know that some things are dangerous. It is also not the case that I am suggesting that we allow children to come to harm. What I am suggesting however is that sometimes a fear of children coming to harm means that we prevent them from encountering anything that might be considered as risky.

This is important if we recognise that if we remove all risks from children's lives we might also prevent the development of both self-esteem and of resilience. In making this claim you can start to see an example of what is meant by criticality within HE. You will often be asked to be critical in assignments and this can sometimes be tricky especially if it is mistakenly presented as finding an alternative perspective. Assignments which take this approach become characterised by Smith (ref) says…. but Jones (Ref) says… You may be familiar with this approach from "A" level studies but there are teachers in Higher Education who promote this also.

What I want to emphasise though is that this is not really what it means to be critical. Being critical is finding faults with theories or practice. It is about finding weaknesses in arguments and in showing what is wrong not just providing an opposite argument. So, in this chapter it may seem perfectly reasonable to remove risk from children's lives until we adopt a critical perspective and recognise that in doing so we are undermining their capacity for development.

This critical approach is useful in illustrating how your studies in Higher Education often require a broad understanding of the issues. For example, it might be that we can offer some simple definitions of some key ideas as are relevant to this book as a whole; what do we mean by: Risk; Vulnerable; Protective; Resilient?

- Risk can be seen as something that can lead to harm; it may be a dangerous element or factor, but it may also be a hazard;
- To be vulnerable is to be capable of being physically or mentally hurt;
- Protective refers to providing or being able to provide protection;
- To be resilient is to have the ability to recover from or adjust to adversity; to be able to bounce back.

That seems straightforward but as a student you need to go further. You need to question the things that you encounter, to interrogate ideas. So, harm may be physical injury but it may also be the fact of low self-esteem in later life. Consider how health and safety falls into this. We tend to be very aware of an immediate risk to safety but are less aware of risks which impact upon health in the future. Think also about who is vulnerable. In Wellbeing, Vulnerability & Life-chances I discussed how it is that we cannot take vulnerability for granted. We shouldn't assume that all children are naturally, or equally, vulnerable. It could be reasonable to suggest that all children are at risk of harm, however some children are more vulnerable to risk due to their environment or due to factors that are unique to them, e.g.

- Being non-mobile; babies under 1 year old are at most risk and the homicide rate is much higher than for older children;
- Disability. If we fail to recognise the additional vulnerabilities faced by some, but not all disabled children, then we are unable to promote resilience;
- Being different in some way, ethnicity could apply here;
- Already being considered to be a problem, such as young offenders or children in care.
-

One other word of caution is required. It is always important to see things as dynamic and to recognise that the risk of harm faced by a child or young person will not remain constant nor will the child's ability to deal with risks. For example, if, as we have said, the child is very young, then the risk is greater. As the child grows older so risk may be lessened. Think about the implications for children with disabilities though if achieving independence is important in reducing risks and if this is impacted on by their disability.

It is also worth thinking about how we understand things as being risky or not. Calder (2008) is useful here. Calder draws on a number of studies to make the point that we are really not very good at assessing risk. This is because we struggle to understand probabilities. We consistently feel that activities over which we have no control pose a greater risk than in relation to those activities where we do have control. The example Calder offers is in driving a car compared to flying. People seem to get very anxious about flying even though statistically it is far safer than driving. This is probably because we feel in control when driving yet what we always fail to consider is that when we are driving we have no control over the actions of other drivers.

It might be worth starting by thinking about how ideas about risk have had an impact upon children's lives. Frank Furedi provides a good example. In recent years Furedi has introduced the idea that parents were becoming paranoid in respect of how they were dealing with their children's lives. Furedi (2001) provides examples of parents going to great measures to oversee the safety of their children such as following a school bus in case it was to have an accident whilst their child was on board. You will probably know of parents who refuse to allow their children to play in their own garden unless they are present to supervise them and watch over them constantly because of stories that have been reported in the press of children who have been abducted. You might even be that parent or have had parenting like this.

These examples illustrate how risk has come to influence parenting. Risk has also had an influence on government policies, what we usually refer to as social policy. For example, Turnbull and Spence (2011) note that "The documentary analysis supports the assertion that 'risk' has underpinned UK Government policy across the field of children and young people since 1996/1997 but not in any consistent manner." (p947). Reading Turnbull & Spence it is evident that some approaches see children and young people being at risk, whereas other approaches see them as the risk! We can also consider that children and young people may be at risk from the actions of others but may also be at risk by engaging in risky behaviour themselves.

This means that there are three ways of thinking about risk:

1. Children and young people are at risk;

2. Children and young people are a risk;

3. Children and young people will do things which are risky.

As a student it is important to be precise when you write assignments. So when you hear someone referring to risk or when you read about risk, especially in relation to children and young people, it is very useful important to be clear which of the three positions listed above applies. In listing these three approaches we can also start to appreciate that risk is not unambiguous. It is not always clear what is being referred to.

2.2 Perceiving risk

If you become, or if you are, a practitioner working with children and young people, there is a need to focus on the types of risky behaviour that children & young people may engage in but that does not mean that children and young people will see things the same way as you do. For example, we can be fairly confident that young people see rock climbing as risky even in spite of the fact that we may argue that no harm will come to them. They may not see smoking as risky even though it is and we can demonstrate that it is. Maybe in these examples we can see how it is that immediacy or delay in experiencing harm impacts upon the extent to which we understand risk. Being aware of the immediate consequences of a fall when rock climbing intensifies the sense of risk about the activity but the long term detrimental effects of smoking reduce the understanding of risk of smoking.

Children and young people are quite capable of understanding the world and drawing conclusions. The thing to be aware of however is that these might not be the conclusions that adults would draw.

In thinking about how adolescents seem likely to engage in behaviours and actions which pose a risk to themselves it has been argued that this is because adolescents seek heightened sensations, they like the excitement. McElwee (2007) however, addresses the claim that adolescence is characterised by "sensation seeking," and argues that this can be rejected as being too simplistic.

McElwee points to how adolescents can be seen to be "actively navigating risky behaviours such as not getting involved in potentially serious physical fights with peers that might involve the use of knives and baseball bats, not using needles to inject drugs, not walking around …. unsafe locations, and, generally using their 'street knowledge' in avoiding situations or people that might pose a threat to them." (p250).This is important because McElwee is able to demonstrate that children and young people are not naïve, something that is often said of them, they are aware of risks. Coleman & Hagell (2007) also note that "for young people risk either involves a degree of chance, or it involves potential harm if precautions are not taken." Importantly, Coleman & Hagell argue that young people consistently refer to personal responsibility when it comes to engaging in risky behaviour.

In thinking about children, young people and risks it may be more accurate to say that at times they both under-estimate and over-estimate them. This idea can be seen in the work of Bond (2013) with respect to mobile phone use.

In reading Bond (2013) it can appear that children and young people display an unrealistic understanding of how mobile phones can offer protection. Think about children and young people as being in a situation in which mobile phones come to act as comfort blankets during a period when the young person is developing confidence in themselves.

However, just as we argued that we should not see all risks as the same, Coleman & Hagell argue that it may be useful to draw the distinction, as we have already done with risk factors, between those which are individual attributes, those which originate from within the family, and those that depend on resources in the neighbourhood or community. At the same time they consider that risk behaviours should also be seen as exploratory. The notion of exploratory risk may be interesting and useful because what we really want is to see children and young people develop in a way which means that they can cope with risks. This is generally referred to as resilience.

As was stated in chapter 1 a simple definition of resilience is the ability of a child or young person to bounce back, to be able to deal with adversity (Frydenberg, 2008). I also put forward the idea however, that there are competing definitions with regards to the construct of resilience. Hamilton (2011) notes that resilience is considered by some to be a characteristic that an individual either possesses or not. For others, as commonly expressed within social work, resilience is a dynamic process and is developed through the interplay of nature and nurture, that is, individual and social influences. As such, viewing resilience in this way, as a process is important for practice as it promotes positive outcomes through interventions.

In respect of the issues that are being covered in this chapter we can see how risks can help young people to discover their strengths, and to enhance self-esteem through overcoming challenges and/or adversity and, in doing so this contribute to the individual's capacity to overcome adversity in the future.

In many ways the resilient child is the child that we would want to produce, the child that we would want to raise. By this I mean that when they have grown up, indeed whilst they are growing up, we would want to be able to reflect upon their development and say that we could be confident that they are able to cope. We may remember though that to develop resilience we need to encounter risk.

That said, I indicated at the start of this chapter that a concern with risk has become very common within society and that this can be seen as shaping practice with children and young people whether that be by professionals and agencies or by parents. For that reason it is useful to consider what is meant by the idea of a risk society.

2.3   The theory behind the idea of a Risk Society

Up to this point I have been talking about how ideas about risk have come to shape children's and young people's lives. In some ways though I may have given the impression that risk is unambiguous. Risk is something which we see as a threat. However, we may also consider, as was suggested at the beginning of this chapter that risk has come to be something which has a major significance on how we understand the world that we live in. There are theorists then such as Giddens, and Beck, who have explained how it has come to be that risk has become so influential in our lives. They suggest that we are living in what we can realistically call a risk society. This has some relevance to how we understand work with children and young people and in terms of the services that are provided for them.

As with many issues relating to children and families you were probably drawn to the course that you have taken because of an interest in children's lives, or in family life. I don't really expect that you have chosen to study some aspect of childhood or family life because of a strong interest in social theory. However, understanding theory will often make you a stronger student because it gives you a bigger picture. Understanding theory means that you can understand the bigger forces that shape childhood, or family life. For that reason, it's worth reading on.

So, for example, in writing about paranoid parenting Furedi, who we came across previously within this chapter is not only describing experiences which apply to children and young people, he is drawing upon an existing body of work which argues that a concern with risk has come to dominate how we live our lives in contemporary society. These ideas can be traced back to two influential theorists writing in the early 1990s. Giddens (1991) *Modernity and Self-Identity,* and Beck (1992) *Risk Society: Beyond a New Modernity* offer a theoretical basis to the idea that society is characterised by a preoccupation with risk. This does not mean that risks did not exist before this time. Giddens is quite clear in arguing that we have always faced risks. For him, it is the way that we now seem to allow ideas about risk and risk assessment to dominate how we live our lives that is important.

Beck says a bit more about how this has come to happen by focusing on the changing nature of risks. So, for Beck a focus on risk has developed because, in many ways, the world that we live in creates risks that are beyond our control. For example, risks posed by nuclear power and pollution are part of the modern world and we can use them to show how things that we rely on often also pose a degree of risk to us. Consider how we know now that lead is dangerous but we once used lead pipes to provide water in our homes and lead was added to petrol to help car engines to run more smoothly. Both provided benefits to us in one way but had a negative effect upon our health. Beck draws upon issues such as these to show how an important aspect of modern life is the way in which the world that we live in creates hazards and risks. So, from this perspective we can say that risk is created as part of the modern world. It is a product of modernization and the shift to a technological world, and this is different when compared to risk being seen as rooted in natural hazards or being seen as in some way fateful.

This requires us to acknowledge though that society has changed and that we can identify this change by referring to modern society and then comparing this to pre-modern society. Think about the difference between the mainly rural society that people lived in before the Industrial Revolution and compare this to the industrial, technological world that we live in now. Risks have changed as society has changed and because of this we can compare risk now to risk in pre-modern societies. In pre-modern societies risk generally came from the natural environment.

Beck is aware however that even industrial society changes. The technologies that we have now are different to the technologies and industry of the mid-18th century for example. We might then draw a distinction again between late-modern, now, and early modern. You may have heard some people refer to post-modern also and I will give a brief explanation of what that is later.

A major problem with risks in contemporary society then, when compared to early modernity is that modern risks tend to be what Beck calls "open-ended" in that they have much wider scope. The Chernobyl nuclear incident in 1986 illustrates what Beck is getting at in that when something like that happens we cannot choose to ignore or avoid it. The Chernobyl incident happened in Ukraine. Its effects however were not restricted to Ukraine. It caused nuclear pollution in the form of radioactivity that was carried across national boundaries by the wind. Debbie Lupton, (2013) shows about how this affected sheep farmers in Cumbria even though the accident happened in Ukraine.

So, risks have changed. For Giddens though the important thing to consider is that it is not that there are more risks in contemporary life, it's just that we seem to be so much more aware of risk. This shapes what we do in terms of how we seem to be constantly assessing risk, both formally and informally, in a way that suggests that we have become averse to risk. We constantly seek to identify it and avoid it. You can see how this brings us back to children and young people in terms of how we provide for them.

So, both Beck and Giddens refer to modernity. What we have seen above is that in a simple sense we can see modernity as a label that differentiates between technological, industrial societies when compared to agricultural and pastoral societies, which we might refer to as pre-modern. Modernity, as a descriptor of a type of society starts with the scientific and industrial revolution but be careful as some theorists now say that we have moved beyond modernity into post-modernity. The thing to take from this is that theorists do not always agree! In fact, the fact that theorists often don't agree contributes to the ways in which we understand risk in that we don't seem to know who to trust anymore. Not knowing who to trust leaves us being uncertain about our lives.

The idea of modernity as being bound up with science and technology corresponds to an optimistic understanding of the modern world. This is the idea that because of science and technology, things will continue to get better. As a society it seems that we are just starting to realise that things cannot always improve. This suspicion is important within the concept of a risk society. What we can see is that in recent years, there has been a growing scepticism about the ability of experts. We might recognise this as being the loss of trust in experts.

2.4 Living in modern society: individual responsibility and choice

Think about what I said above about modernity. This may give a sense of what modernity looks like but it doesn't tell us what living in modernity feels like. Elliott and Lemert (2014) provide a good summary of what Giddens says about modernity and refer to him claiming that modernity is like a juggernaut that is out of control. We are constantly experiencing social change in ways that are beyond our control. Hartmut Rosa (2013) develops this idea further and argues that modernity can be characterised by an increasing pace of life, something that we often hear being said about life. The modern world is a fast-paced world.

So, for Giddens, we are living in a world that is characterised by constant social change and we are faced with risks which emerge from modernity. However, alongside this, Giddens points to a concept that is seen as important in understanding social life: the concept or practice of reflexivity: a concern with self-reflection. You will often come across this idea in respect of reflective practice. For Giddens reflexivity is an essential part of social life.

We naturally reflect upon the world that we live in and consider where, and how, we fit in. However, in contemporary society this process has been significantly intensified. So, we can see that reflexivity becomes something that is not just what individuals do, it becomes a social practice in that we are expected, or required, to do it.

What this means for society is that we come to see our lives as a project that we manage. We reflect on who we are, what our life is like and then by considering the resources available to us we project manage our lives to achieve goals, (Ferguson, 2003, D'Cruz et al., 2007). This sense of planning our own future is something that is very new. As an example, think about how often you, as students, are advised to do things, or acquire skills and experience, so as to make yourself more employable. Ask grandparents who were your age in the early 1960s if they ever thought about employability skills, I would expect them to ask you what you mean.

We can also see how this sense of reflexivity becomes entwined in all aspects of our lives such as reflecting upon the extent to which you are a good mum or a good friend etc. Within this reflective approach though is an inevitable element of self-blame. It is individualistic; problems become your problems rather than being seen as social conditions. What we can see is that there has been a significant move towards reflexivity and that this is often bound up with ideas about accountability. In turn this reflects a much more individualist account. Garrett (2018) has argued that this is embedded within the political ideology of neoliberalism.

A key aspect of understanding how reflexivity shapes our concerns with risk can be seen by turning our attention to what we can call individualisation. By this we are saying that we become much more concerned with ourselves as individuals. Our understanding of our self as an individual can be seen to have been heightened as things which can be seen as having bonded us together in previous generations have broken down. For example we can see in the increase in single-parent households that the family has changed and although we might still see the family as important it is not as tight knit as it once was. Similarly when we think about how social class impacted upon our lives in previous generations or how we gender was experienced then we can see how social life seems much more flexible now. The old bonds can be said to have broken down and we have become much more individualised.

This breakdown in more traditional forms of social systems is said to have increased both anxieties and responsibilities for individuals. Think about how it was that for a long time working class boys in particular would follow fathers into industrial occupations and women were always seen primarily in terms of being housewives. This sort of world has gone and the need to define our own future becomes the prime motive for many but it often means that it is pursued at the cost of commitments to others and this has the effect of further weakening social ties. It is supported though by the increased practice of being reflective, of reflecting upon who we are and what we want our life to be. So, if we agree with Beck and Giddens that we have become much more reflective, and agree to call this reflexive modernity then we can start to see where contemporary society impacts upon our lives in a way that heightens our sense of risk.

Alongside this is the growing prominence in our lives of the idea of choice. The situations that we find ourselves in, are often seen as being the consequences of the choices that we make but this is a poor explanation really. Debbie Lupton (2006) illustrates this by referring to debates around the case of IVF in Australia. She shows how, in contemporary society, social changes which have led to more women staying in education longer and pursuing careers, or marrying later, results in many women not wanting to get pregnant until they are in their late 30s or into their 40s.

However, what we do know is that it is harder for women to get pregnant at an older age. This is a biological reality. It is easier to get pregnant at 23 than it is at 43. When women cannot get pregnant it becomes recast, not as the consequences of social changes which have led to many women deferring pregnancy, but as the consequence of individual life choices. Please do not see this as an argument from me that women should not stay in education or pursue careers, it is simply an example of a particular consequence of social change.

Personal or individual choices often loom large in discussions of risk but they often do so in a way which ignores the social context. So, what we find is that in any society, there are some things which are understood as being risky and other things which are not. Do an internet search for "Human towers" and look at the Catalan tradition of building human towers which end with quite young children climbing to the top without a safety harness. Consider how many parents in the UK will not to let their children climb trees, a very popular pastime when I was a boy, but will happily strap their children into a vehicle that they will then drive at quite excessive speeds and sometimes in a dangerous manner. Can you see how the issue of control comes to the fore again?

2.5 Explaining risk and the risk society

If we think back to what was covered earlier I said that to understand childhood it is important to consider the social, cultural and political context within which a child lives. That is because these three factors all act to shape how a child experiences life. I said also that if a child is to develop and maintain resilience it is important that they encounter adversity within their life so that they can develop approaches to deal with it. I also ended by considering how young adults are often referred to as snowflakes and wondered if any inability of young adults to handle adversity or criticism could be a consequence of being sheltered from it whilst growing up. Consider how children are being metaphorically wrapped up in cotton wool to protect them by over-protective parents and think about how parental fears about risk may be the one thing that makes their children more vulnerable and less resilient.

If you end up working with children and young people you will often be called upon to assess risks and there is much evidence to demonstrate that concerns about risks have led to children being restricted in what they can do or in terms of what we provide for them. Wheway (2007) provides lots of examples about how Health & Safety concerns are employed to reduce risks. For Wheway (2007) however, it is important to consider the nature of each because what we might recognise is that they have different concerns, concerns which may be contradictory. For Wheway what stands out is that very often safety takes precedence over health. That is worth thinking about. What he is saying is that anxieties about safety lead to restrictions being placed on what children can do, and which very often means they live sedentary lives, in ways which may have significant consequences for their health as adults.

In terms of social, cultural and political issues you may want to draw upon the model that was presented by Bronfenbrenner, (1979). In Bronfenbrenner's model the child is at the centre but they exist within a series of contexts which Bronfenbrenner represents as concentric circles. This is a very useful model for getting us to consider the ecology, or the environment, of the child. The child's experiences are, to a large part, shaped by others. If the outer ring represents society and society is preoccupied with risk it can be seen how the rings that are nearer the child are influenced by what is happening in society in general. This takes us back to examples provided earlier of parents restricting what their children can do or where they can go because of anxieties about risk, (Creasy and Corby, 2019, Guldberg, 2009, Jenkins, 2006).

This may be a good time to return to the debate within sociology of approaches that rest upon structure, and those that rest upon agency. This is because on the one hand I have suggested that society has become more individualised and that this rests upon individual choices and behaviours; and on the other hand I have pointed to the ways in which social structures provide the context for this individualisation. We are, of course, concerned with what this means for children, young people and families so I will point to issues that are relevant to those.

In terms of structure we can say that socio-cultural practices and policies, along with social diversity and social divisions act as structures within which the child lives. In terms of agency we are considering those behaviours that the child chooses such as how they spend their free time and with who, although we might consider that this is not entirely free and that it changes with age and independence.

In considering how parents come to wrap their children up in cotton wool we inevitable look for influences upon their lives. One important factor, though not necessarily a driving factor, is the media. Think what Lupton (2006) is saying when she says that "Blame is also often a key aspect of media coverage of risk" (p17). Is she pointing to the way in which accidents and tragedies seem to be approached by the media with a concern to apportion blame. Interestingly she also comments that "…media attention to a risk issue does not necessarily translate into concern on the part of lay audiences." (p18). In part this reflects the idea that ordinary people have become more skeptical about experts. If media attention to an issue does not necessarily translate it into a concern we might consider that there are some wider forces at work.

2.6 Where do I fit this in?

To end this chapter I will do the same as I did for chapter 1 and will pick out some key points that I think would be expected in an assignment about risk. As before, I am not saying that these are the only important points because your assignment might want something very specific. As I said in chapter 1 then always read your assignment guidance carefully and take advice about what will attract higher marks. You probably have marking criteria which try to define what an assignment that receives a 2:1 or a 2:2 will look like. Marking criteria are very difficult to write in a way that is totally unambiguous so you have to see them as guides rather than fixed definitions. For example, if the criteria for your assignment says that to be awarded a 2: 2 mark your work has to be good, what does good mean? Does it mean every part has to be good? What this really means is that the advice I gave in chapter 1 about the need for clear writing stands. Always give lots of time to proof reading before submission. Never see a submission date as the date when you have to finish your assignment, it isn't. The submission date is when it has to be submitted by. Always aim to complete the assignment at least one week before that so that you have a few days to proof read.

However, having said why it is important to write well my real concern here is with the content. So, for me an assignment on risk really ought to make the point that:

- Risk refers to something that can lead to harm. This could be physical injury now but it could be a problem that is only evident much later such as poor health;

- Risk has come to play a major part of practice with children and young people;

- We need to experience risk as part of our development. If we remove all risks from children's lives we will hold back the development of both self-esteem and of resilience;

- Risk is dynamic. The risk of harm faced by a child or young person will not remain constant nor will the child's ability to deal with risks;

- We often see risk as lower when we are in control and higher when we are not in control;

- Risk has shaped social and public policy relating to children and young people;

- We might see children and young people as being at risk, as being a risk, and as doing things which are risky;

- Risk factors may originate in the individual, in the family, and in the community;

- Some social theorists have suggested that a concern with risk has shaped society to such an extent that they refer to "risk society";

- Risk society contributes to increased individualisation and a sense that we have to project-manage our own lives.

Depending on the course that you are on you might find that some of the issues covered in this chapter are more useful than others. Some courses will emphasise risk in more practical terms such as risk assessments whereas others will be more critical and will want to evaluate the ways in which risk shapes how we go about our lives and what this means in providing for children and young people. So, be careful in what you choose from this chapter. Don't write an assignment to a different question! It happens. I always think that considering context is important but if you are asked for something very specific then provide something very specific. The next chapter will be useful if you have an assignment which asks you to explore the consequences of risk and the ways in which we may go about providing for children and young people facing risks in that it looks at safeguarding. Inevitably though it will draw a distinction between safeguarding and child protection and consider the political context in which this may change.

3 SAFEGUARDING

3.1 A child in need, and a child being harmed: culture & values

So far I have put forward arguments which indicate that it is important for children and young people to have resilience so that they may cope with adversities in the future. I have also suggested that a growing concern with risk has impacted upon the lives of children and young people in terms of what they are able to do and that this is counterproductive with respect to developing and maintaining resilience. That said, there are children and young people who do face adversities of a kind that they really should be protected from. Because of this I now move on to consider a number of issues regarding how society safeguards children and young people from risks. The aim is to provide students with an understanding of issues related to safeguarding and child protection so that you may understand the ideas and concerns which underpin safeguarding and so that you might write about them more effectively.

Let's start this chapter though by drawing a distinction between safeguarding and child protection. The first thing to establish is that safeguarding is much broader than child protection. So, it may be more accurate for you to recognise that child protection is an aspect of safeguarding. This returns us to something that I have said before in that as a student it is always important to be precise when you write. Think carefully about the words that you use. This can be seen as returning to the importance of discourse, especially in terms of the language that we use to describe things and how this shapes our understanding. Consider the following example from May-Chahal & Coleman (2003: XV). May-Chahal & Coleman avoid the term 'Child abuse', preferring instead to use 'child maltreatment' and significant harm'. They offer three reasons for this:

- Most European countries reserve the use of 'abuse' for cases of sexual abuse, having other terms that approximate to 'maltreatment';

- 'Child abuse' suggests that there is a proper use for children reflecting ideas about ownership;

- 'Child abuse' may be seen as too general as it has come to refer to a range of 'harms' as well as behaviours which sometimes lead to no harm at all.

It is worth reiterating however that providing detailed descriptions of a range of terms is beyond the scope of this short book. My aim with this book is to get you to think about principles and to introduce to critical ideas about such principles. There are other books which are much for focused on the details. Lindon et al. (2016) for example provide a very accessible discussion of safeguarding including good descriptions of the range of issues involved.

When it comes to safeguarding it is fairly clear that safeguarding and/or protection is required in cases relating to the maltreatment of children and young people. Such maltreatment may range from physical and sexual abuse to neglect. The Children Act 1989 introduced the test of significant harm as being the trigger in respect of intervening to protect children. This sounds straightforward; if a child or young person is experiencing significant harm then there is a duty to protect them. As with some other concepts that I have introduced previously though the act is not as clear cut as it first suggests. The problem is that the Children Act did not define what significant harm is and practitioners are required to make a judgement about the extent to which the child is likely to be harmed and the possibility of such harm continuing. A good account of the Children Act is provided by Holt (2014). Another useful summary of the ideas which underpinned the Children Act that is very accessible is Griffith (2009). As before, full details are in the reference list.

May-Chahal and Coleman (2003) make a good point in relation to this. They draw attention to how we might distinguish between a child in need, and a child being harmed. This distinction makes more sense by considering some previous guidance from the DfES (2006) which identified three domains within which issues may arise that see the need for safeguarding actions to take place. This meant that practitioners at the time were being asked to consider information and analysis relating to:

- the child's developmental needs;
- the parents' or caregivers' capacity to respond appropriately to those needs;
- the wider family and environmental factors.

You will often come across the term, the "toxic trio" in respect to safeguarding. It refers to the way that children are deemed to be at greater risk if their home life involves parents with mental health issues, substance abuse such as drug taking, and if there is violence such as domestic abuse. The toxic trio is useful in demonstrating how concerns with keeping children and young people safe have moved beyond a concern with direct actions against the child. The toxic trio encourage us to consider the context within which the child lives in a way which acknowledges that the social context can shape the personal experience.

However, as Morris et al. (2018) demonstrate, although the term "toxic trio" has become commonplace within social work practice there is a danger that it restricts thinking about safeguarding to characteristics of the family and of the idea of toxicity itself rather than what is leading to harm. Morris et al. (2018) point to wider structural factors such as the harms posed by poverty and deprivation. Featherstone et al. (2017) also make a good case for considering the wider context.

This is a good time to return to a point that was made previously about the way in which some things look obvious. We can look at the three domains, or three aspects of a child's life above and think that they are obvious, that they are unambiguous, but are they? We could consider the extent to which we really know what the child's developmental needs are, or to consider the extent to which we can say that parents or caregivers are able to respond to those needs. Then we have to think about the wider family or environmental context (remember Bronfenbrenner's concentric circles?).

Now think about how difficult it is for practitioners to remain objective at all times yet that is what is required of them. Fontes (2005) raises an interesting point relating to child abuse in the USA which addresses this. She notes that although there are no significant differences in incidences of maltreatment between African Americans and White Americans, African Americans are more likely to be accused of maltreatment and to have this upheld in investigations. This then has the consequence of seeing children removed from the home. Think about how this might be as a consequence of ideas that are held about some social groups. For example, she talks about how boundaries are established in families and how some families have very fixed or rigid boundaries and others are more flexible. Her discussion of the flexible boundaries that can be seen in many poor or ethnic minority families is interesting as it reveals how diverse practices can be understood within a cultural context. In the UK Featherstone et al. (2017) point out that children from deprived communities are far more likely to be removed from the family than are children who live in wealthy communities.

With this in mind think about your own values and beliefs. Can practice be separate from values and beliefs? I am going to put to you that it is not really reasonable to suggest that practice can develop in a way that is totally separate from our values and beliefs. We can be critical of the society that we live in and I have urged you to be critical as you read this book but it is not always easy. Some things just seem unquestionable. Practice changes because of factors such as policy change, political direction and funding. In turn though this impacts on our opinion of what is acceptable or not.

In relation to child protection you may also come across the idea of 'thresholds'. To define thresholds is to suggest that we can define a point at which a child is more or less at risk. You may also be exposed to the term 'good enough' parenting. This again aims to define a standard of parenting that will ensure a child develops sufficiently and will not suffer harm despite the absence of things that others may take as essential such as a lack of material possessions, or a lack of educational ability of the parents. It may also apply where there is the presence of behaviour that some would find difficult to tolerate such as drug and alcohol use. When we think about it there is often nothing inevitable about thresholds or about what is seen as being good enough. These come to be established in a way which means that they act as tools which enable practitioners to operate in their jobs. They are not fixed though. They can change.

So, as an example consider practitioners working with parents where drug use is evident. Let's say that it is you that is part of a team sitting around a table at a multi-agency meeting sharing information regarding a family and looking at how the child and family can be best supported. A decision has to be taken about the risk posed to the child by the parents drug use. 'Drugs' can be seen as a major risk to the safety of the child. As a worker you may feel that any drug use suggests these parents are unfit to appropriately care for their child. You may be right, however let's consider knowledge, values and beliefs.

How knowledgeable are you on the impact of drugs on behaviour? How knowledgeable are you on the habits and behaviours of these parents in terms of drug taking?

What value do you place on such things as 'sobriety', 'abstinence', 'drunkenness'? In fact what value do you place on the role of the parent in respect of their own needs?

What are your beliefs regarding drug taking? What are your beliefs about people who take illegal drugs?

Sometimes professionals have to develop the ability to set aside their own values and beliefs and accept that others can lead different lives to what they may experience and yet still be 'good' parents. I am not saying that this is always true but I want you to think that it is possible.

3.2   Keeping children and young people safe from themselves

If we go back in time, to the 1970s there was a strong tradition of work with children and young people which emphasised child protection. This is one of those things which seems obvious on first reading especially in a culture where we are often being reminded that children are naturally vulnerable. The focus of child protection was on identifying those children deemed to be at risk and working, or intervening, to prevent this. After 1997 and the election of the Labour Government under Tony Blair, this focus on child protection can be seen to have been replaced by a concern with safeguarding. What you will often read is that this was as a consequence of one particular case relating to one particular child; Victoria Climbie'. Victoria Climbie' was murdered by her aunt and her aunt's boyfriend in February 2000. It was a case which came to dominate what was happening within children's services at the time and for some time afterwards.

In moving from a focus on child protection to a focus on safeguarding though we need to recognise that the ideas which underpin each also change. In child protection the child is at risk from the actions of specific adults. Very often this was seen as family members. The focus therefore is quite narrow. It is on particular children at risk from particular adults. In safeguarding the risk is shared by all children. All children can be harmed and all adults can be the threat. In this approach we all come to be seen as a potential threat and we all come to have responsibility for keeping children safe. We can see this in the introduction of Criminal Record Bureau checks (CRB) came to be used in ways that restricted how adults could interact with children and young people. CRBs were required to work with children and young people but they also came to represent safety in a way which also meant that anyone without a CRB was to be seen as a potential threat. CRBs have since been replaced with the Disclosure and Barring service check (DBS).

In the shift from child protection to safeguarding there is also a further aspect that is certainly worth considering. Child protection always seems to reflect ideas about others being a threat to children, usually adults. In terms of safeguarding there is a much broader approach being taken and this shows us how the introduction of new policies changes how we see things.

The Victoria Climbie' case is often presented as being the catalyst for a policy framework called Every Child Matters. In 2003 the Labour Government published a plan for a new policy approach that was aimed at improving the life experiences of young people and children: *Child Matters: Change for Children (ECM)*. This policy document highlighted the need for a comprehensive revamp of the services available to children, young people and their families. Four key themes were at the centre of this initial green paper which endeavored to strengthen preventative services. These were:

- Increasing the focus on supporting families and carers;

- Ensuring necessary intervention takes place before children reach crisis point and protecting children from falling through the net;

- Addressing the underlying problems identified in the report into the death of Victoria Climbié, said to be weak accountability and poor integration;

- Ensuring that people working with children are valued, rewarded and trained.

The Labour approach termed Every Child Matters can best be understood as a framework which shaped how practitioners working with children carried out their work. It was a framework which shaped how Ofsted carried out inspections and it strongly influenced the Children Act (2004). Overall, it did much to shape how practitioners engaged with, and provided for, children. For example, the introduction of the Criminal Records Bureau (CRB) check, replaced in 2012 by the Disclosure and Barring Service (DBS) check reinforced the idea that all adults posed a threat unless they were certified as safe through undertaking this official check. Every Child Matters introduced five key outcomes which were widely adopted across services working with children, one of which was "Stay safe" and although Every Child Matters was effectively shelved in 2010 when the Conservative led Coalition government came to power it can still be said to have some influence today. A very good discussion of what Every Child Matters was can be found in Knowles (2009).

The value of Every Child Matters can be seen in how it put forward five outcomes that should be worked towards in terms of children and young people. The aim was that every child (0-19 years), whatever their situation or background, will have access to the support required to:
- Be healthy
- Stay safe
- Enjoy and achieve
- Make a positive contribution
- Achieve economic well-being

These five themes then were established as the principle goals that Every Child Matters set out to achieve. As a consequence agencies and practitioners could be seen to organise and evaluate themselves in terms of the five outcomes. In turn this was encouraged by Ofsted inspections which assessed how schools and Children's Centres met these outcomes.

The Every Child Matters framework had a significant influence on practice especially with respect to safeguarding. As is established above one of the 5 outcomes of Every Child Matters was Staying Safe. The influence that this had however was on the way that practitioners turned their focus on to making the environment safe and how this included becoming increasingly aware of how children's own behaviours may serve to create risk.

To explore this idea further it would be easy to look at how children and young people take part in risky behaviours such as substance abuse which, for example, might include drinking alcohol and smoking cigarettes. At the same time there is legislation in place to restrict children and young people's sexual activity, ostensibly to protect them from themselves as well as from others. In recent years though there has been concerns raised about how children and young people use technology, something that is becoming deeply embedded within the everyday lives of children and young people. With this in mind, the following section addresses some aspects of technology. Concerns about technology and how children and young people use it are heightened to an extent by the widespread adoption of smart phones and the way in which this provides easy access to the internet.

What you might want to consider then is how IT and media have created a modern day risk that is difficult to address especially by parents who feel ill-equipped to understand just how the internet has come to be used. What is ironic when we think about the idea of the internet posing a risk to children and young people is that the fear of the risks that are said to be all around us in society overlaps with contemporary ideas about what it means to be a good parent and this leads many parents to confine their children to the home, where they very often turn to technology. In other words we may see how it is that risks which parents can understand create the conditions by which children and young people are more likely to encounter the risks that parents do not understand.

3.3   Sex, technology and risk

In the last couple of decades there has been a growing concern regarding the idea that children and young people need to be protected in respect of sexual activity. This is not entirely new as most countries establish an age at which young people are deemed to be able to give consent to engaging in sexual activity, (Moore et al., 2018). In some ways the ideas that underpin a sexual age of consent reflect ideas about development and what can be called age-appropriate behaviour. Having an age of consent indicates a belief that children and young people either cannot make rational decisions regarding natural human behaviours prior to a particular level of development or that they constitute a socially weak group who require protection from older members of society. Maybe it is both! However, one thing which demonstrates the extent to which these ideas are social in nature rather than being somehow natural or obvious is that there are significant differences regarding what the age of consent should be and what it is.

So, just as we have argued that discourse can shape our understanding of the world that we live in we might consider that legal structures can do the same. How we approach protecting and safeguarding children may be shaped by values and beliefs which are found within discourses regarding sexual behaviour and which underpin legal structures but where the legislation becomes taken for granted.

To illustrate how social attitudes differ and change try to find out what age Elvis Presley, a revered musician, was when he met his future wife and how old she was. The Tate is an art gallery and many art galleries show nudes in paintings and photographs. In September 2009 however, the Tate removed a picture of the actress Brooke Shields posing nude. She was 10. In Shakespeare's Romeo & Juliet how old is Juliet? Looking at cases such as these demonstrate that ideas about what is appropriate change.

Many teenagers engage in sexual activity which is illegal because of the age of consent but what is illegal in the UK may not be illegal elsewhere. Similarly we can draw a distinction between consenting behaviour between two 15yr olds as illegal but not abusive.

But look at how ideas about what is right or wrong can come up against the law. In 2015 a 17 year old boy from Fayettville, North Carolina, was charged with possessing child pornography when his phone was found to contain photos of himself naked. In 2014 Nottinghamshire Police warned under 18s that they could be placed on the sex offenders register for distributing child pornography if they shared nude photos that they had taken of themselves, (Guardian, 2014). Currently in the UK 16 year olds can legally engage in sexual activity, but cannot legally possess nude photos of each other as this constitutes child pornography. Now consider also that in UK law individuals can marry at 16.

The relevance of these examples is in the fact that typically we have tended to assume that children face risks from others who will treat them in ways that can cause them harm. What we must also consider is that children's behaviour may be risky in itself and therefore children & young people may pose risks of harm to themselves in varying ways. Alongside this the practice of sexting or taking nude selfies illustrates how the world that we live in may create new risks, (Megele and Buzzi, 2018, Moore and Reynolds, 2018). The invention and mass adoption of mobile phones with the capacity to record still and video images, together with the possibility of instantly distributing such images has created this "new" danger that young people face. The Protection of Children Act 1978 is legislation which makes it an offence to take, make, show and/or distribute indecent images of children. This predates mobile phone and email technology.

It's not my intention to be a luddite here and I am not arguing that New Technologies have created new behaviours rather that they have the ability to change behaviours in ways which increase the risks that young people face based upon consensual behaviour.

In respect of legal definitions of minors re indecent images a child is seen as below the age of 18 as a consequence of the Sexual Offences Act 2003, which extended the Protection of Children Act 1978 to cover indecent photographs of children aged 16 and 17. The Act also introduced a new set of offences specifically dealing with the exploitation of children though child abuse images, providing protection for all children up to the age of 18. You can find Crown Prosecution Service information regarding indecent material online at https://www.cps.gov.uk/legal-guidance/indecent-and-prohibited-images-children. Note that the definition of a child was altered from 16 to 18 years' by section 45(1) of the Sexual Offences Act 2003, in force from 1 May 2004. Of course, depending upon when you read this, it may have changed again. Always be careful to check details when it relates to the law.

The possession of indecent images and videos of minors can lead to imprisonment and being recorded on the Sex Offenders Register. If we consider the increase in practices such as sexting we can see why it is that most sex offenders are under 25.

The advent of mobile phones incorporating digital cameras and video recorders together with Internet resources such as social networking sites (such as Facebook and instagram) and webcams have also opened up new avenues for bullying and new risks, (Megele and Buzzi, 2018). Not only can indecent and embarrassing images and videos be posted on the net, mobile phones and social networking sites provide a range of opportunities for the posting of malicious texts and comments.

Though privacy settings and the ability to block numbers seem sensible ways of avoiding the experience of cyberbullying it may be that the best approach is caution. Remember also that organisations such as Schools, Care homes and Colleges have a duty of care to safeguard young people. Take a moment however, because at this point it might be worth considering your own cyber-presence. Before we are critical of young people's use of the internet consider how you might have used the internet and what material might someone be able to find about you. Now think also that employers have been known to search the internet in relation to applicants for jobs and that some people have lost their jobs because of the material that they have posted on sites such as Facebook. For example, consider the case of Rachel Burns from 2015, (McDermott, 2017).

In one sense cases about the internet and about social media usage point to the way in which safeguarding can be seen as a more useful approach towards providing for children and young people than is child protection. Although I am cautious and critical about the actual extent of threats it is the case that if we only focus on physical threats we are very likely to miss some children who are experiencing other types of harm. But, to repeat something that I have said before, when we want to understand the ways in which we provide for children and young people and when we want to make sense of how children and young people experience their lives it is important that we take a broad perspective. If you are to write good, academic assignments you are usually going to be drawn into considering the social, cultural and political contexts within which children and young people live. This is something that the next section says more about. In one sense it may appear to be moving away from the actual issues that children and young people face but it is very important to understand if we are to understand childhood.

3.4 Making use of this in assignments

It's perfectly reasonable to imagine that you will take a module on safeguarding and child protection and once again you might find that you are being asked to consider very specific issues such as legislation and details about practice such as what to do if you suspect a child is being abused. I have avoided that level of detail. My concerns are always about developing an understanding of safeguarding overall. This will include how child protection fits in and it will consider the political dimension to this. So, as always, think about the key points that I would expect to see in an assignment on safeguarding but see them as suited to an assignment that is broad. If your task is very specific use what you need. For me though I think it will always be important to consider that:

- Child protection is an aspect of safeguarding. Child protection tends to be very focused on children identified as being at risk of being harmed. Safeguarding is a much broader approach that covers all children;

- The Children Act 1989 introduced the test of significant harm as being the trigger to intervening to protect children but did not specify what significant harm is;

- The Every Child Matters framework did much to bring safeguarding to the fore;

- The "toxic trio" of parents with mental health issues, substance abuse, and violence are important in safeguarding practice;

- Safeguarding practice will require an understanding of values;

- We may safeguard children from others and from themselves;

- As new technologies develop they may create new risks which require changes to how we safeguard.

You can probably see how safeguarding follows on from risk but safeguarding could also be seen as more likely than other aspects of work with children and young people to be subject to political change. Think about how child protection emerged in a focused way and then became much broader as part of the Every Child Matters agenda. This means that you might have to be more careful when it comes to assignments because this is one area where you might be tied to particular aspects. However, if the political context of safeguarding is important or interesting to you read section 4.1 in the following chapter. If it's not, even though I think that it is really interesting, you might just skip to section 4.2 looking at how you might understand the book as a whole as a lengthy essay.

4 THE SOCIAL AND POLITICAL CONTEXT

4.1   From Child Protection to Safeguarding (and back again?)

I started this book by considering debates around the concept of resilience. I argued that we all need to develop resilience and that we need to maintain it. Resilience is not something we either have or do not have. It is not something that that can be used up. It's always best to see resilience on a continuum and to recognise that how resilient we are can change throughout our lifetimes. Importantly though I argued that children need to experience adversity if they are to develop risk and I provided the analogy of inoculations in which we are given a small amount of a disease so that our body can develop immunity to that disease.

Chapter two then went on to discuss the issue of risk and demonstrated that as is often the case, risk is not unambiguous. By that I mean we cannot see it as being either black or white. Recognising that many social issues are not black or white is very important when studying issues relating to children, young people and families, and this is something that, as students you really need to get a hold of. If you have recently undertaken school or sixth form studies such as "A" levels there is often a strong sense that there is always a right answer. As you study social sciences in Higher Education you often find that this is not the case and that it is very important that you are able to craft a good argument.

Although it is clear that some things present clear and obvious dangers many risks are far less certain. Because of this we need to accept that risk is very often socially constructed especially in terms of how we respond to what we perceive as risky. Chapter two also put forward the ideas of Ulrich Beck (1992) in particular in saying that a concern with risk has come to dominate modern life to the extent to which it can be said that we are living in a risk society. This has consequences for our everyday experiences especially with regards to what children and young people are allowed or permitted to do and this will impact upon resilience to some extent.

So, as was indicated in chapter 1, we can understand resilience as being developed and maintained in the relationship between the individual, the family and the community. However, I indicated that this always takes place within a social context and following from theories of risk society it is possible to recognise how adversity comes to be portrayed as risk. Following from this it becomes easy to see how a concern with risk aversion will influence family and parenting practices creating parents who are risk averse. What this means for children is that they often experience significantly less exposure to adversities than in previous generations. This means that children's everyday lives are changed in a way that restricts their opportunities to develop resilience. In a broader sense risk is presented as being something which children cannot cope with or understand. In turn this has an impact upon how parents come to view themselves in that a good parent is a parent who removes adversity from children's lives. In Creasy and Corby (2019), Fiona Corby and I argue that this leads to a tame childhood and that this is not in anyone's interests.

For example, what we can often see then is that one particular characteristic of a preoccupation with risk is the proliferation of restrictions on what children can and cannot do. Previously, I pointed to how equipment, games and activities have all come to be restricted on the grounds that they pose a potential danger to children, (Wheway, 2007). When we consider this alongside the idea that children are naturally vulnerable as was considered in Childhood: Wellbeing, Vulnerability and Life-chances we can start to see how children's lives have been subject to increasing control and how this has seen children having much less freedom than in previous generations. As is always the case though the ideas which come to shape any society or culture do not just emerge, there are factors and events which shape them.

The case of Victoria Climbie' was very important with respect to how safeguarding developed in the UK but we could ask why it was that this case changed things when there were very many cases of children being harmed and even killed before this. Read Parton (2004), the details for all references are listed below in the reference list. Parton offers a good account of how social change can be seen as the context for the shift from child protection to safeguarding by looking at an equally distressing case from the 1970s, that of Maria Colwell. In one sense what you see when you read Parton is that he is suggesting that particular cases come to be seen as emblems of particular social problems. As such they act as triggers or catalysts for changes to the existing system. What Parton also does though is to turn our attention to the social context within which systems such as children's services operate.

So, with this in mind I want you to think about two aspects of social change that are relevant, and which you can explore further by locating and reading Parton. The first is social change and how this has had an impact upon the family. The second is political change and how this has changed the context within which we understand social services.

So, when it comes to the family Parton demonstrates how the social context of families has become quite complex and diverse. With respect to the political context, politicians who promote the ideas of neoliberalism have done much which contributes to a reduction in trust in such as social workers and have contributed to change to the way that they work. For example, in a paper about the death of another child, Peter Connelly, often referred to as Baby P, Joanne Warner (2013) talks about how social workers come to be seen as uncaring, working to a tick-box system. It would be wrong of us to think that Social Workers have in some way decided amongst themselves that this is how they will work. It would be better to consider the extent to which how they work has been changed by others. One way of understanding this is to see how they work as having been changed by something that is often referred to as a managerialist way of working. In turn, managerialism is something which can be seen as being driven by neoliberalism, (Creasy, 2018).

So, what we must always consider then is that to understand something such as practice with children, young people and families, it is important to consider the social, cultural, and political context at the time. As such we might see how the Climbie' case provided an opportunity for the Labour Government from 1997 to establish that they had a different approach to the neoliberal influenced Conservative governments led by Thatcher and Major. So, it might not be that this case is particularly different, or that it is particularly shocking. It might just be that it happens at the right time for any particular government; in this case, the Labour Government.

If you read Childhood: Wellbeing, Vulnerability and Life-chances you will have a good idea about the basic arguments and principles of neoliberalism. If you didn't read Childhood: Wellbeing, Vulnerability and Life-chances another good introduction to neoliberalism, and how it shapes managerialism is Creasy (2018). As a very basic summary we can say that neoliberalism promotes individualism alongside ideas about self-responsibility arguing that society is always served best when individuals can pursue their own interests within a free market. What this tends to mean is that neoliberal governments generally seek to cut social services or social support because they see welfare services as bad for society. For neoliberals the free market is the best way to provide for society's needs.

However, although neoliberals promote the free market over all other forms of social organisation there are few doubts that free markets lead to widening inequalities. What is important to note here though is that neoliberals do not see inequalities as a problem. From a neoliberal point of view inequalities are the cumulative consequences of the individual choices that we, as individual make. Because of this, neoliberals resist arguments which explain inequalities as being rooted in social characteristics such as social class, gender or ethnicity. From a neoliberal perspective, individuals will do well if they are talented and work hard, and they will not do well if they lack abilities or do not work hard. They resist any arguments which suggest that prejudice or discrimination impacts upon inequalities and will tend to gloss over arguments which point out that having advantages from childhood contributes to being advantaged later in life.

During the 1980s and 1990s the neoliberal governments led by Margaret Thatcher and John Major were often accused of being uncaring because of the way in which they cut support for social services. Thatcher in particular was criticised for a comment she made saying that there was no such thing as society (foundation, 1987). So, if the neoliberal inspired Conservative governments from 1979 – 1997 are arguing that there is no such thing as society here is the basis of the key difference between them and the Labour governments under Tony Blair. We can see this in two things which are particularly relevant to children, safeguarding, and the approach that came to be known as Every Child Matters.

Think about this. Thatcher and Major were criticised for apparently not being bothered about many people in society, especially the poor. In one sense, the Labour Party under Tony Blair needed to demonstrate that they had an alternative vision for society, a society whereby the government were concerned with everyone. In terms of what we are concerned with in this series of books we can start to see how, under Blair's New Labour government, the policy framework which came to be presented as Every Child Matters promotes the idea that the government are bothered about all children. This suggests a much more inclusive approach and clearly responds to Thatcher in saying that there is such a thing as society. But, what also changes is that we move away from a system in which some children at risk, as in child protection, and we see the introduction of an approach whereby all children are at risk and safeguarding is everyone's responsibility. What's more risk itself comes to be a much broader concern and is no longer confined to threats to children which are rooted within the home and/or from family members.

In this way, the political perspective of the government at the time, in this example, the Labour Government who are adopting a much more inclusive approach than previous governments, is manifest, or made real, in the way that it establishes a policy framework which influences society in a wide-reaching manner. The key thing for you to take note of here is that things do not just happen with respect to how we provide for children and young people. It is always important to consider the social and political context within which developments can be seen to take place. So, the move away from safeguarding and back towards child protection, with its greater concern about individual children, rather than all children, can be understood in the context of the change of government in 2010 and the return to power of a more explicitly neoliberal government.

4.2   This book as an essay

As a book this is far longer than any essay you are likely to be asked to write but don't think about the length, think instead about the structure. When you write an essay you should always have a clear structure and the structure should always enable you to develop a clear argument. See your essays as an argument on paper where no-one is butting in. It's just you making your point.

So, let's imagine I was given an essay title something along the lines of "Why is resilience important and how do social issues impact upon it?" OK, I've cheated in that I have written a title question that fits with what I have already written about but that's not too unrealistic. I can't remember the last time I gave students an essay title. I always take the approach that coming up with a good title is all part of the challenge so my students tend to write their own. That means that you get more flexibility because you know what interests you. Not all students get this choice and in some professional degrees there can be good reasons for specifying a title. But if we did have this title how have I responded to it?

The first thing I did was to say how resilience is important in terms of achieving wellbeing to set the scene (be careful not to see this as the introduction, an introduction always outlines the structure of the essay) and then I went on to define what I mean by the term resilience. That gave me the opportunity to demonstrate understanding by pointing to resilience as being slippery and it means that I can drop in a few references for different approaches. Importantly I talked about it being seen as a trait compared to a process. I also put forward a process view as the preferred view.

From that I looked at what can support the development and maintenance of resilience. This though gave me an opportunity to make the point that we need adversity to develop resilience and I took the opportunity to consider if those young people referred to as snowflakes were young people who had been protected from adversity. In doing that I set myself up to say that if we want to understand resilience we ought to consider the way in which risk has become very prominent with society.

So I explored the ways in which we can understand risk. We can see immediate risks such as safety concerns, we can see deferred risks such as consequences for health. I could have dropped in an example of parents confining children to the home and how this seems to protect them from immediate risks in the community but subjects them to potential health risks because they end up sat on computers or even facing online risks such as online grooming.

I also raised the matter of risks being dynamic and showed how some risks diminish as we get older. This meant I could drop in a comment about vulnerability and that demonstrated understanding of wider issues. It also meant dropping in a few more references.

Play the game! Show that you have read some books.

After defining risks I went on to say how risk has become prominent in social life and how government policies have incorporated ideas about risk. This meant I could should the broader context of risk. I talked about children and young people recognising risks and navigating risks but I then demonstrated my understanding of how social theory fits in by talking about risk society and reflexivity. From this though I brought it round to saying that if we can see resilience is influenced by ideas about risk it makes sense to consider social and political responses and therefore I introduced a discussion of safeguarding.

Again, I had to offer some definitions and this usually gives an opportunity to show how there can be ambiguities or tensions in terms of how we use language. I also illustrated how values and cultural practices have real consequences for some children and families. I indicated how we had seen a widespread concern with safeguarding arise with the political framework set up in Every Child Matters (it may have been scrapped but it had real impact for practice). I then went on to consider technology as a specific example and showed how safeguarding and the law can appear to be contradictory. So, as an essay it just needs me to tie these up in a conclusion by saying something like we would want children and young people to develop resilience because that contributes to their wellbeing. However, the social, cultural and political context of their lives may mean that they have more or fewer opportunities to do this. So, if we consider how society appears to have been preoccupied with risk and how this has led to some significant and far reaching practices aimed at safeguarding we might recognise that if we seek to remove all adversity from children's lives then we are not helping them in the long run.

Of course, you would have fewer words so you are likely to need a stripped down version but the structuring of the argument is what is important. Build it up and support your points by providing evidence. The evidence is the references that you use and this means that you will have to read a lot. You can't get around that.

4.3   What to do next

I hope that this has been helpful. This is one of a number of short books that aim to provide a critical and theoretical introduction to key issues relating to studying childhood, and associated courses such as Children, Young People and Families or courses linked to social work. It is aimed at those students within Higher Education who are currently working with children and/or young people, or those students in Higher Education who intend to work with children and/or young people. There are some who may still think that theory and practice are separate; that in the real world it is what we do that is important not the theory. This is not the case, that what we do, what you do, practice, is shaped by both theory and politics which is why there is theory and politics throughout the book.

See it as a starting point to develop understanding but you have to read widely afterwards. The final thing in this book then is something that some students overlook. Don't. What comes next is really useful when it comes to how you can demonstrate engagement with your studies and how it could support the things that you will write about. It is, of course the reference list. When I was a student, before computers and before the internet finding books and journal articles was nowhere near as easy as it is now and my go-to source was always the reference list in the books and journal articles that I did get hold of. I always thought, "if it's good enough for the author, it's good enough for me!" My advice is to get hold of some of the sources that I have used and have a read. Some will be challenging but that is not a bad thing at all.

REFERENCES

BECK, U. 1992. *Risk society: towards a new modernity,* London, Sage.

BOND, E. 2013. Mobile phones, risk and responsibility: Understanding children's perceptions. *Cyberpsychology.*

BRONFENBRENNER, U. 1979. *The ecology of human development: Experiments by nature and design,* Cambridge, MA, Harvard University Press.

CALDER, M. C. 2008. *Contemporary risk assessment in safeguarding children,* Lyme Regis, Russell House.

COLEMAN, J. & HAGELL, A. 2007. *Adolescence, risk and resilience: against the odds,* Chichester, John Wiley.

CREASY, R. 2018. *The Taming of Education,* Basingstoke, Palgrave.

CREASY, R. 2020 *Wellbeing, Vulnerability & Life-chances*

CREASY, R. & CORBY, F. 2019. *Taming childhood?: a critical perspective on policy, practice and parenting,* Basingstoke, Palgrave Macmillan.

D'CRUZ, H., GILLINGHAM, P. & MELENDEZ, S. 2007. Reflexivity, its Meanings and Relevance for Social Work: A Critical Review of the Literature. *The British Journal of Social Work,* 37, 73.

DFES 2006. What to do if you're worried a child is being abused. *In:* DFES (ed.). Nottingham: DfES publications.

ECCLESTONE, K. & LEWIS, L. 2014. Interventions for resilience in educational settings: challenging policy discourses of risk and vulnerability. *Journal of Education Policy.*

ELLIOTT, A. & LEMERT, C. 2014. *Introduction to contemporary social theory,* Abingdon, Oxon, Routledge.

FEATHERSTONE, B., GUPTA, A. & MORRIS, K. 2017. Bringing back the social: the way forward for children's social work? *Journal of Children's Services,* 12, 190.

FERGUSON, H. 2003. Welfare, social exclusion and reflexivity: the case of child and woman protection. *Journal of Social Policy,* 199.

FERGUSSON, D. M. & HORWOOD, L. J. 2003. Resilience to Childhood Adversity: Results of a 21-Year Study. *In:* LUTHAR, S. S. (ed.) *Resilience and Vulnerability:*

Adaptation in the Context of Childhood Adversities. Cambridge: Cambridge University Press.

FLETCHER, D. & SARKAR, M. 2013. Psychological resilience: A review and critique of definitions, concepts, and theory. *European Psychologist.* Germany: Hogrefe Publishing.

FONTES, L. A. 2005. *Child abuse and culture: working with diverse families,* London, Guilford.

FOUNDATION, M. T. 1987. *Interview for Woman's Own ("no such thing as society")* [Online]. Available: https://www.margaretthatcher.org/document/106689 [Accessed 17 September 2019].

FRYDENBERG, E. 2008. *Adolescent coping: advances in theory, research, and practice,* London, Routledge.

FUREDI, F. 2001. Paranoid Parenting. *The Guardian.*

GARRETT, P. B. 2018. *Welfare words: critical social work & social policy,* London, Sage.

GIDDENS, A. 1991. *Modernity and self-identity: self and society in the late modern age,* Cambridge, Polity P.

GRIFFITH, R. 2009. Safeguarding children: key concepts and principles. *British Journal of School Nursing,* 4, 335-340.

GUARDIAN, T. 2014. Teenagers who share 'sexts' could face prosecution, police warn. *The Guardian.*

GULDBERG, H. 2009. *Reclaiming childhood: freedom and play in an age of fear,* London, Routledge.

HAMILTON, W. 2011. Young people and mental health: resilience and models of practice. *In:* O'DELL, L. & LEVERETT, S. (eds.) *Working with children and young people: co-constructing practice.* Basingstoke: Palgrave Macmillan.

HOLT, K. 2014. *Child protection,* Basingstoke, Hampshire, Palgrave Macmillan.

JENKINS, N., E. 2006. 'You can't wrap them up in cotton wool!' Constructing risk in young people's access to outdoor play. *Health, Risk & Society.*

KNOWLES, G. 2009. *Ensuring every child matters,* London, CA, SAGE.

LINDON, J., WEBB, J. & LINDON, J. 2016. *Safeguarding and child protection,* London, [England], Hodder Education.

LUPTON, D. 2006. *Sociology & Risk* [Online]. Researchgate. Available: https://www.researchgate.net/publication/265568289_Sociology_and_risk [Accessed 16/09/2019 2019].

LUPTON, D. 2013. *Risk,* Abingdon, , Routledge.

MARTÍNEZ-MARTÍ, M. L. & RUCH, W. 2017. Character strengths predict resilience over and above positive affect, self-efficacy, optimism, social support, self-esteem, and life satisfaction. *The Journal of Positive Psychology.* United Kingdom: Taylor & Francis.

MAY-CHAHAL, C. & COLEMAN, S. 2003. *Safeguarding children and young people,* London, Routledge.

MCDERMOTT, S. 2017. *I lost my job over a Facebook post - was that fair?* [Online]. BBC: BBC. Available: https://www.bbc.co.uk/news/stories-41851771 [Accessed 03/11/2019 2019].

MCELWEE, N. 2007. Chapter 9: Framing the Future for Children and Youth in the Risk Society. *Child & Youth Services,* 29, 249-268.

MEGELE, C. & BUZZI, P. 2018. *Safeguarding children and young people online: a short guide for social workers,* Bristol, England, Policy Press.

MOORE, A. & REYNOLDS, P. 2018. Sex, Sexuality and Social Media: A New and Pressing Danger? *In:* MOORE, A. & REYNOLDS, P. (eds.) *Childhood and Sexuality: Contemporary Issues and Debates.* London: Palgrave Macmillan UK.

MOORE, A., REYNOLDS, P. & SPRINGERLINK 2018. *Childhood and Sexuality: Contemporary Issues and Debates,* London, Palgrave Macmillan UK.

MORRIS, K., MASON, W., BYWATERS, P., FEATHERSTONE, B., DANIEL, B., BRADY, G., BUNTING, L., HOOPER, J., MIRZA, N., SCOURFIELD, J. & WEBB, C. 2018. Social work, poverty, and child welfare interventions. *Child & Family Social Work,* 23, 364-372.

OLSSON, C. A., BOND, L., BURNS, J. M., VELLA-BRODRICK, D. A. & SAWYER, S. M. 2003. Adolescent resilience: a concept analysis. *Journal of Adolescence.* Elsevier Ltd.

PARTON, N. 2004. From Maria Colwell to Victoria Climbié: reflections on public inquiries into child abuse a generation apart. *Child Abuse Review,* 13, 80-94.

ROSA, H. & TREJO-MATHYS, J. 2013. *Social acceleration: anew theory of modernity,* New York, Columbia University Press.

TAKET, A. R., NOLAN, A. & STAGNITTI, K. 2014. Family Strategies to Support and Develop Resilience in Early Childhood. *Early Years: An International Journal of Research and Development.*

TAYLOR, Z. E., EISENBERG, N., SPINRAD, T. L. & WIDAMAN, K. F. 2013. Longitudinal Relations of Intrusive Parenting and Effortful Control to Ego-Resiliency during Early Childhood. *Child Development.*

TURNBULL, G. & SPENCE, J. 2011. What's at risk? The proliferation of risk across child and youth policy in England. *JOURNAL OF YOUTH STUDIES -ABINGDON-.*

WARNER, J. 2013. Social work, class politics and risk in the moral panic over Baby P. *Health, Risk & Society,* 15, 217-233.

WHEWAY, R. 2007. Not a risk averse society: Fair Play For Children. 2 ed. Bognor Regis: Fair Play for Children.

INDEX

Finally

Many thanks for reading this, you are welcome to provide feedback and/or suggestions via my email address:

robcreasy@hotmail.co.uk

If you do want to get in touch you might provide a brief response to the following questions:

- Overall, was it useful? Is there anything that I should add or change?
- Have I got the tone right, is it too deep or not academic enough?
- Does it speak to you, does it make sense?

I do have a favour to ask though. I decided to self-publish this book because the prices that major publishers charge can be prohibitive. By self-publishing I can sell this, and other related books as referred to, for a small amount but that means that I don't have a marketing budget. So, two things will really help me:

1. Please recommend this book to friends;
2. Please leave a review on Amazon, having lots of good reviews in particular is really helpful.

Best wishes, Rob.

ABOUT THE AUTHOR

Dr Rob Creasy was previously Director of Social Sciences at York St John University in the UK. He has taught in Further Education and Higher Education for over 30 years. He is the author of "The Taming of Education" (2018) published by Palgrave Macmillan and the co-author of "Taming Childhood" (2019) also published by Palgrave Macmillan as well as a number of journal articles. He wasn't all that good at school and got his first "O" level aged 25. His undergraduate and postgraduate degrees are in Sociology, Social Policy and Education and he is a Senior Fellow of the Higher Education Academy. In 2015 he led the introduction of BA Sociology at York St John University; in 2019 this was ranked as the number 1 sociology course in the UK based on student satisfaction as reported in the National Student Satisfaction survey.

Printed in Great Britain
by Amazon